Beyond Broke

**Empowering Your Finances
in the Face of Bills**

JASON MART

Beyond Broke:

Empowering Your Finances in the Face of Bills

Copyright © 2023 by Jason Mart

Table of Contents

Dedication

To my wonderful wife,

You remained by my side with unshakable support and love at the darkest of times, when the burden of uncertainty weighed heavy on my shoulders. Even when the road appeared to be impossible, it was your perseverance and faith in us that kept me going. Your unfailing support while I was completely broke was a ray of hope and proof of our unbreakable friendship. You are my pillar, my source of hope, and my most priceless possession. You are my constant source of resiliency and strength, and this book is dedicated to you.

Introduction

There is a cliche in the personal financial and business worlds that goes, "You have to hit rock bottom to rise to the top." Because I've experienced it myself, I really believe that proverb. Welcome to my story of going from being totally jobless and bankrupt to being a successful business owner.

I recently found myself in a circumstance that many of us hate and fear: losing a reliable employment. My formerly taken-for-granted sense of security disappeared, forcing me to struggle with uncertainty and financial difficulty. To put it mildly, it was a trying experience, and I felt as though I were perched on the edge of an abyss.

But as you can see, there are times when our full power and potential show themselves in those moments of despair and suffering. I didn't want to be defined by my circumstances. Instead, I made the decision to see my unemployment as a chance—a chance to reinvent myself and pursue my passion.

I had long had the desire to launch my own company, and this unanticipated setback served as the impetus for its accomplishment. I entered the field of entrepreneurship with the belief that I could build something worthwhile and long-lasting.

The path to business ownership, nevertheless, wasn't without its difficulties. I experienced betrayals, financial difficulties, and the devastating impact of losing dependable staff members. These difficulties put my willpower and fortitude to the ultimate test. Nevertheless, every obstacle and betrayal served as a teaching moment for tenacity and flexibility.

I'll describe my harrowing path from being jobless and broke to becoming the proud owner of a successful company in the pages that follow. Along the road, I picked up insightful knowledge about leadership, financial empowerment, and the value of sticking with my goals even when the going became tough.

Whether you're battling your own financial difficulties or following your business aspirations, my aim is that my experience will encourage you.

Always keep in mind that hardship is not always the start of a tremendous development. It's an honor to be able to share my knowledge and perspectives with you, and I cordially encourage you to go on this path of empowerment and fortitude with me.

Chapter 1
Embracing Financial Reality

New York City, they say is "the city that never sleeps." the city where fortunes are gained and aspirations are realized. It's a city where towering buildings strive for the stars and the streets throb with life. It exudes energy, ambition, and unrelenting motion. It's a place where everyone may succeed, a city of opportunity and optimism.

With aspirations as lofty as the Empire State Building, I traveled to New York City. I was ambitious and wanted to rule the world when I was just out of college and had a marketing degree. It seemed like the first step toward attaining those goals to land a job in the city. I was prepared to embrace the activity, difficulties, and potential of this iconic place.

For a while, city life lived up to my expectations. I had a reliable work at a marketing firm, a small apartment in a bustling area, and friends who shared my enthusiasm for life. I was buoyed by the vivid spirit of the city and sure that I was headed in the right direction.

But life has a tendency of catching us off guard, and these shocks can occasionally be unpleasant.

It all began with a meeting at work, one of those dreaded events where you can tell something is wrong as soon as you enter the conference room. My gut tightened as the phrases "budget cuts" and "restructuring" reverberated across the room. My position was one of many lost in the company's downsizing. The wonderful job I had fought so hard for was gone in a flash.

The days that followed were a haze of uncertainty and bewilderment. The city, which had previously seemed like a playground, now appeared to be a cruel maze. An unending round of job applications and interviews took the place of my typical day of office meetings and client presentations. I had the impression that I was putting my CV into a black hole and would never hear back from employers.

Months passed into weeks, and my bank account was depleting quickly. I had just enough money for pocket change after paying rent, groceries, and other necessities. I stood there helplessly as my funds vanished and my feeling of security was eroded by the city's unrelenting cost of living.

Recognizing My Current Financial Situation

Debts started to mount like frightening storm clouds. My inbox was overflowing with notices of unpaid rent, school loans, and credit card bills, all of which served as reminders of my financial predicament. My self-esteem suffered as a result of the creditors' constant requests for payment, which turned into a daily agony.

I was sinking in a sea of debt, and no matter how hard I tried to remain afloat, I couldn't. To make money meet, I sold priceless belongings, pawned jewels, and even accepted odd jobs. But it was like attempting to use a teaspoon to save a drowning ship. The bills kept growing, and I felt like I was being crushed by the weight of my financial situation.

The truth struck me like a freight train one especially dreary evening as I glanced at a stack of overdue invoices and thought about the mountain of debt that hung over me. I was actually, clearly broke, not just temporarily inconvenienced. It wasn't a setback; rather, it was an enormous financial disaster. When it came to paying off my debts, my salary couldn't even begin to meet my essential living expenditures.

The reality of my financial situation weighed heavily on me as I sat in the poorly lit room, and I came to the realization that I could no longer run from the fact. I had to stop putting off answering my creditors' calls or holding out hope that a job opportunity would arise out of nowhere. No matter how intimidating or uncomfortable it might be, I had to face my financial realities head-on.

Accepting financial reality is similar to standing on the edge of a cliff, gazing into the distance, and realizing that you are on the verge of being bankrupt. It's a difficult self-awareness moment where you must face the decisions and circumstances that have brought you to this place.

But it's also a turning point where you realize you have a choice, a moment of clarity. You have two options: either you take charge of your financial future and set out on the path to a brighter future, or you may keep your head in the sand and hope that things will somehow magically get better.

I was aware that I was at a crossroads and needed to make a choice. No matter how unpleasant or humiliating it might be, it was time for me to confront my financial realities. It was time to go along a route that would take me from being broke to having financial security and, eventually, wealth.

The Decision to Change: A New Beginning

A spark of resolution ignited within me as I gathered the invoices and bank records strewn across the table. I would face my financial realities and do whatever it required to get through this obstacle that seemed insurmountable. I was prepared to face the challenging path ahead with an open mind and unwavering commitment.

I came to the realization that the first step on this road was to face my financial realities head-on in a concrete way as I sat there, surrounded by the outward signs of my financial suffering. I had to paint an accurate, truthful image of my financial situation. I thus started to compile all of my financial records and invoices, something I had been putting off for far too long.

They were there, each envelope telling its own story of debt, like a threatening army of paper soldiers. I carefully organized them into tidy heaps according to their due dates after sorting them. The bills' digits glared back at me in an accusatory and harsh manner. It was a frightening sight, but it was also one that was required.

I couldn't help but recall a lesson my grandmother used to teach me as I sorted the paperwork: "Face your troubles head-on, dear, for that is the only way to overcome them." As I looked at the stack of bills, Grandma's statements that she had been a smart woman resounded in my head.

Now that I had my papers in order, I started making a thorough inventory of all my debts. It was a wake-up call. I included all of my creditors along with their current balances, minimum monthly payments, and interest rates. A knot in my throat developed while I was adding up the statistics. The whole debt exceeded my expectations and appeared to be overwhelming.

However, there was a strange sense of relief when I realized how bad my financial situation really was. I had been living in a denial fog, and now that the fog had gone, I could plainly see my predicament. Although it was a terrible truth, it was also the catalyst for transformation.

I was aware that just recognizing my obligations and their size would not be sufficient. I needed a strategy—a road map—to get me through this treacherous terrain. I then began to look into debt management and financial recovery options.

I once came across the tale of a lady who had faced financial devastation but had been able to turn her life around while searching the internet for help. Her story was both motivating and enlightening. She had used a technique called the debt snowball method.

Regardless of interest rates, the debt snowball strategy entailed paying off debts one at a time, starting with the lowest and moving up to the largest. To develop momentum and drive early in the process, it concentrated on achieving little triumphs. On my path to financial recovery, I was intrigued to the notion of recognizing minor victories.

With this newfound understanding, I made the decision to design my own debt snowball strategy. I sorted my obligations according to their magnitude, starting with the smallest. It was a concrete action that provided me a sense of control—something I really needed.

I then started to evaluate my monthly spending. I needed to make a realistic budget that would enable me to pay for my essential expenses while also allocating funds to pay down my debts. I carefully tracked my expenditures, made cuts to wasteful spending, and gave priority to necessities.

I couldn't help but identify places where I had been overspending when I looked through my budget. Regularly eating out, having several streaming subscriptions, and making hasty purchases were all bad behaviors that had led to my financial ruin. I was resolved to make changes that were obviously required.

My financial reality had to be accepted, which was liberating and sobering at the same time. I had accepted the reality of my predicament, made a plan to deal with it, and was now making strides toward financial recovery. Although it wasn't an easy path, it was one that was motivated by hope and willpower.

I was aware that I was not the only one going through this as I kept working on my strategy. There were numerous others who had overcome financial hardship and come out stronger. I used their tales as beacons of hope to help me get through the worst of my financial problems.

Although the path beyond broke was difficult, it was also paved with opportunity for learning and development. It was a voyage to eventual financial security and wealth. And it all started with the straightforward decision to accept my financial realities.

Chapter 2
The Financial Rat Race

Finding a new job that paid more than my previous ones was really exciting. It was a new beginning, a ray of optimism after months of unrelenting job searching and unstable finances. On my first day, I entered the office with a fresh feeling of hope and purpose. I had no idea that the weight of past debts and rising expenses would continue to loom large over my life.

I was resolved to make good use of the increased income that came with the new job. But the burden of mounting debts brought on by my earlier financial difficulties continued to be terrible. The interest rates on credit card bills, school loans, and past-due medical bills seemed to grow, making the climb out of debt seem unattainable.

With little room left for financial independence, each paycheck that entered my account seemed like a little triumph before the debt monster ate it. In my life, the phrase "rat race" acquired a new significance. No matter how much money I made, it always seemed like I was chasing my financial tail, trying to keep up with the escalating costs.

During the time I was unemployed, I had picked up a lot of worthwhile knowledge. I developed my ability to stick to a budget, be thrifty, and maximize every dollar. I learned the value of having an emergency fund and the painful consequences of not having one. The most important lesson, though, was realizing how simple it was to rack up debt and how difficult it might be to escape that pit.

Despite the priceless lessons I had learned through my financial difficulties, it appeared that I was still lacking a crucial component of the jigsaw. Even though I was aware of sound financial principles and intended to put them into practice, the burden of mounting debts proved to be a tenacious foe. But the reality of bills forcefully activated my mind to find a way out.

Taking up new side jobs and extra work
Innovation frequently results from desperation, and I was determined to stop the pattern. To

increase my income, I started looking into several side businesses. I took on freelance tasks in the evenings and on the weekends, making use of the abilities I had developed over the years. The additional employment supplied more than just extra money; they also gave people a fresh feeling of direction and purpose.

I started to reap the rewards of my additional work. The money made from side jobs was used to pay off high-interest obligations. Although it was a difficult and sometimes arduous process, I felt a rising feeling of satisfaction and control over my financial future with each debt milestone I hit.

Importantly, I was aware of my financial difficulties and realized I had to make a major shift in order to stop the pattern. I started investing in building quality relationships in addition to other tactics in order to increase my possibilities and seek out more money. I looked for chances to network with new individuals. I went to social events, networking functions, and neighborhood meetings. These events gave me the possibility to meet people who might be able to introduce me to side jobs or business prospects in addition to helping me widen my social network. I realized how crucial it was to provide value to others in order to gain their friendship. I made an effort to make a positive difference in the lives of everyone I came into contact with, whether it was via sharing my knowledge, offering my time and abilities, or just listening well.

Chapter 3
From Broke to Empowered

The journey was not as easy as one imagining himself on a different plane financially from his realistic present level. Undoubtedly, I would lose practically everything on this adventure. It was a voyage that nature had planned to change not just my finances but also, and perhaps more crucially, the way I think in general.

How can one transition from feeling completely broke and overwhelmed to feeling in control and empowered in terms of finances? was my query. I was aware that the solution required not only practical strategies but also a significant shift of mindset.

Shifting Your Mindset for Financial Success

It's frequently stated that acknowledging you have a problem is the first step toward addressing it. I had undoubtedly admitted to my financial situation, but that wasn't sufficient. I have to think differently. I needed to shift my perspective from one of being a victim of circumstance to one of being the designer of my financial destiny.

I started by changing the way I thought about money. I began to see money as a tool—a tool that could be utilized to create the life I desired—instead of as a cause of stress and scarcity. I was able to approach financial decisions with a feeling of purpose and goal because to this mental adjustment, which was essential.

Allowing myself to let go of guilt and shame over my financial condition was one of the most effective mental changes I ever made. When you're buried in debt, it's simple to point the finger at yourself, but obsessing on past mistakes just leaves you mired in a cycle of self-loathing. I came to the conclusion that in order to move on, I would need to forget about my past financial mistakes and concentrate on making wiser decisions going forward.

I began searching for financial education to help me maintain this new outlook. I consumed personal financial books, went to workshops, and listened to podcasts. I came to see that knowledge was a powerful remedy for anxiety and uncertainty. I felt more empowered to manage my financial future as I learned more.

The Power of Mindset

Our mindset or mentality is a strong influence on how we think, believe, and behave. It serves as the filter through which we view the world and make sense of our experiences. Our mindset is crucial in defining our financial well-being in the area of personal finance.

Consider this: You are more likely to engage in self-destructive financial practices if you think you will always be penniless and that money is elusive and exclusively for the fortunate few. You run the risk of overspending, accumulating debt without a strategy to pay it off, and abdicating any financial responsibilities. This negative outlook turns into a self-fulfilling prophesy.

On the other hand, you are more likely to make sensible financial decisions if you embrace an attitude of financial empowerment. You'll take initiative in managing your finances, making financial objectives, and looking for ways to increase your wealth. You are set up for financial success with this approach.

Why Your Mindset Matters

Our mindset determines our financial actions and decisions, which accounts for where we are financially. This is how it goes:

Beliefs Drive Behaviors: Your financial decisions are influenced by the way you view money. You're unlikely to save if you think it's meaningless since you'll always have plenty. You will lose out on the chance to develop your money over the long run if you think investing is too risky.

Self-Fulfilling Prophecy: Your mindset has the potential to become a self-fulfilling prophesy. If you are consumed with fear of financial failure all the time, you can end up making choices that put you in financial difficulty. However, a positive outlook can result in proactive financial behaviors and successful consequences.

Risk Tolerance vs. Risk Aversion: A mindset of fear and shortage often leads to risk aversion. You forgo chances or investments that may increase your money out of a fear of losing what little you already have. An attitude of plenty and empowerment, on the other hand, advocates taking sensible risks and making investments in your financial future.

Response to Setbacks: Financial setbacks are inevitable in life, but how you react to them depends on your perspective. Negative thinking may result in hopelessness and passivity, whereas positive thinking fosters resilience and the will to overcome setbacks.

Changing Your Mindset

Although it's difficult, changing your thinking is necessary for financial empowerment. You may change your thinking to achieve financial success by following these steps:

Self-Awareness: Start by becoming aware of your existing financial mindset. Do you frequently hold unfavorable opinions regarding money? Do you frequently feel helpless or overwhelmed? The first step toward change is realizing where you are.

Challenge Limiting Beliefs: Identify any limiting assumptions you may have around money and put them to the test. Consider if these views are supported by facts or are only assumptions. Is it real that you'll never have enough money, for instance, or is it a fear-based assumption?

Affirmations: Incorporate some affirmations about money into your everyday routine. Remind yourself frequently that you have control over your finances, that you make wise financial decisions, and that you are able to succeed financially.

Be Positively Surrounded: Surround yourself with people and things that support financial empowerment. Participate in books, podcasts, and online groups that highlight financial success stories and strategies.

Set Goals: Establish goals that are in line with your changed mindset on money. Having clear goals offers you a feeling of direction and purpose, which reinforces your confidence in your financial ability.

Continuous Learning: Dedicate yourself to continual financial education. You'll feel more comfortable making financial decisions as you gain more knowledge about personal finances, investments, and wealth-building techniques.

Practice gratitude: Develop an attitude of thanksgiving for all of your possessions, no matter how little they may be. Gratitude encourages an optimistic financial mentality by shifting your attention from scarcity to plenty.

Keep in mind that changing your perspective on money is a continuous process. Be patient to yourself and acknowledge minor accomplishments along the road. Your mentality is what's driving your financial path, and by adopting the appropriate attitudes and ideas, you can change your financial reality from one of scarcity to one of empowerment and abundance.

The Building Blocks of Financial Empowerment

I was prepared to build the groundwork for financial empowerment after changing my mindset. I understood that in order to protect my financial future, there were several key building blocks I needed to put in place.

Budgeting

A well-structured budget is the basis of every

sound financial strategy. I was aware that I had to have a thorough awareness of my earnings and expenses. I started keeping track of every dime that came in and went out after that, equipped with spreadsheets and resolve. Seeing where my money was truly going opened my eyes. I eliminated unnecessary expenses and came up with strategies to reduce my expenditure without lowering my standard of living.

Emergency Fund
Having a safety net is essential for financial security. A three-to-six-month emergency fund was the minimum amount I wanted to accumulate. Without turning to credit cards or loans, this cushion gave me a sense of security and enabled me to weather unforeseen financial storms.

Debt Repayment Strategy
I made paying off my debt a high priority. I adhered to my debt snowball strategy, paying off the smallest balance first and transferring the monies saved to the next bill. Each loan that was paid off was a minor accomplishment that increased my self-assurance and motivation.

Savings and Investments
I understood the value of conserving money for the future in addition to how important it was to pay off debt. I started investing in low-risk securities and transferring a portion of my salary into a retirement account. This proactive mindset provided me a feeling of purpose that went beyond my current financial difficulties.

Continuous Learning
I committed to continuing my studies in finance. My confidence in making wise decisions increased as I learned more about investing, taxes, and financial planning.

I could feel the change taking place inside of me as I placed these foundational pieces of financial empowerment. I was actively involved in my financial achievement rather than just being a passive observer of my financial problems. Although it was a slow, up-and-down process, there was undoubtedly a progressive motion.

The Entrepreneurial Dream

My entrepreneurial spirit started to burn brightly when I had a strong grasp of money and managed my debt well. I had always had a secret yearning to launch my own company, waiting for the proper opportunity to manifest.

With my financial condition getting better, I saw a chance to make that goal a reality. I had an idea for a business that would enable me to follow my passion and do something valuable in addition to being a source of money.

I now possess a fresh feeling of resolve and ingenuity thanks to my experience going from being broke to empowered. It was time to put the skills I had gained about money management, saving, and budgeting to use by starting my own business.

There were still more obstacles to conquer, lessons to be learned, and preparations to be made, though, before I could start my business path. Aside from that, I was still somewhat free of my debts, and I knew the path ahead would be unclear, but I had faith that I could get beyond any financial difficulties that were in my way.

I knew my entrepreneurial dream would be a reality in the nearest future when I was full grounded with the insights and experiences garnered along the way.

They were more to learn...

Chapter 4
Creating a Financial Blueprint

The development of a thorough financial plan was a crucial stage in the transformation from broke to empowered. It was the time when my hopes and goals materialized into a clear strategy that would direct my financial choices and activities. This chapter examines how to create a thorough budget and establish **SMART** financial objectives which forms a bedrock in creating a financial blueprint.

Crafting a Comprehensive Budget
Making a budget involved more than simply keeping track of expenditures; it also involved creating a financial road map that would help me reach my goals. To make sure that every dollar was being used effectively, it entailed carefully examining my income, costs, and spending patterns.

Understanding My Income
In order to create a thorough budget, I had to first determine my income. I included my salary,

freelancing earnings, and any additional cash streams in my list of sources of income. I was able to see my monthly cash flow clearly as a result of this.

I then kept meticulous track of my spending. To organize my expenditures, I looked over my bank and credit card statements, as well as receipts. It was a painstaking procedure that demanded close attention to detail, but it was crucial in helping me find places where I could reduce wasteful spending.

I categorized my expenses into two main categories:

Fixed Expenses: These were monthly expenses that were predictable month to month. Rent, utilities, insurance, and loan payments were among them. Fixed costs were necessary and could not be avoided.

Variable costs: Variable costs were more adaptable and could be changed in accordance with priorities. They included spending categories including those for food, eating out, entertainment, and extracurricular activities.

I started making a budget when I had a good idea of my income and spending. This budget has to be practical and in line with my financial objectives. Here's what I did to approach it:

- I broke down my spending into categories, each of which represented a different area of my life. Housing, transportation, shopping, leisure, savings, debt repayment, and more categories were covered.
- After creating the groups, I divided my money among them. Since fixed expenditures could not be negotiated, they were given priority. My aims and financial objectives guided how I distributed variable costs.
- I set aside a chunk of my budget as my beginning capital for a future business. This financing would be crucial in helping me realize my entrepreneurial goal.
- I built a contingency category into my spending plan to cover unforeseen costs and revenue variations. This made sure I was ready for the unpredictability of life.

Setting SMART Financial Goals

Making a thorough budget was an essential first step, but it was just one aspect of the process. I needed specific, doable goals in order to maintain my drive and attention throughout my financial journey. My efforts were motivated by setting SMART financial goals.

Specific: SMART objectives were clear and precise. I make concrete objectives instead of just saying, "I want to save money," such as, "I want to save $10,000 for my emergency fund within 12 months."

Measurable: Keeping on track required tracking progress. I created specific measures to assess my progress toward my objectives. For instance, I kept an eye on the amounts as they decreased to measure my debt repayment progress.

Achievable: Realistic and reachable within my financial means, my goals were. I set myself high goals, but I also made sure that they were attainable via hard work and discipline.

Relevant: Each objective I selected was pertinent to my overall monetary well-being and matched my beliefs and priorities. This made sure I stayed dedicated to them.

Time-Bound: SMART objectives have deadlines. To create a sense of accountability and urgency, I established deadlines for each objective. This avoided procrastination and offered a precise path to achievement.

Long-term and short-term goals

I had both short- and long-term financial goals. Building my emergency fund, paying off certain debts, and accumulating startup capital for my firm were among my short-term objectives. In the short term, these objectives gave us a sense of accomplishment and advancement.

My whole financial approach was dictated by long-term objectives including gaining financial independence and building a diverse investment portfolio. They served as the impetus for my attempts to create long-term wealth and safeguard my financial future.

Envisioning Success

In order to achieve my SMART financial objectives, visualization of achievement was a useful tool. I made vision boards, used graphs and charts to measure my progress, and celebrated accomplishments along the way. This tangible example of achievement inspired me and served as a reminder of the benefits I would eventually reap from this financial path.

I knew that discipline and tenacity would be my best allies as I made progress with my financial plan. The budget would act as my financial compass, and SMART objectives would act as my guiding lights, illuminating the path to a more promising financial future.

Chapter 5
The Journey to Financial Independence

With a marketing degree and many employments in marketing companies, I started my path to financial freedom. I found myself in a comparable position at a different company after leaving my first job. I was resolved to excel in the position since I was accustomed to it. I had been working hard to learn new things, hone my talents, and be ready for a better future during the time between employment.

I worked my way up the corporate ladder throughout the years, using what I had discovered. But even as I rose, I couldn't get rid of the impression that my financial development was no different than drawing water from the sea with a cup. I realized there had to be a better method to safeguard my financial future despite my knowledge and commitment.

The art of forming connections and adding value to others was one important lesson I learned over my career. These abilities played a significant role in my life, assisting me in developing relationships that would be useful in the long term. I found that these connections were very satisfying on an emotional level as well as professionally.

I was an authority in my area and had perfected the art of selling without really "selling." I realized that the key was to interact with individuals, ascertain their needs, and provide answers rather than simply selling stuff. This strategy was not only effective but also in line with my ideals, which made my job even more satisfying.

Nevertheless, despite my successes, I still felt the need for more. Given what I had learnt, I was aware that my income potential was far more than what I was now making. Insatiable want for unrestricted money in the future drove me to take risky actions in that direction.

My entrepreneurial spark was rekindled one day. I made the decision to use my marketing expertise to launch my own company. It was a risky decision with a fair amount of uncertainty, but I was driven by a burning desire to take charge of my financial future.

I looked to the excellent connections I had made over the years. Friends and relationships that I had made as a result of my commitment to helping others. I contacted them and explained my goals for launching a company. I carefully planned each stage of the route and created persuasive recommendations.

I faced many obstacles on the way to financial independence, but I never wavered in my commitment to overcome them. I used my knowledge, my contacts, and my willpower to develop a company that would not only give me financial stability, but also satisfy my entrepreneurial passion.

I found myself in a position where investors were prepared to participate in my potential business endeavor as my plans to launch a firm started to take form. They were interested in me because of my years of marketing experience and track record. These doors of opportunity were greatly facilitated by the contacts I had built over time.

The ability of the investors to manage the complexities of marketing, as well as my vision and industry knowledge, piqued their interest. They were excited to see my company concept take off because they saw its potential for success.

Days were set aside for presentations, in-depth conversations, and more explanations of the business plan and its potential for expansion.

It was, to put it mildly, a promising endeavor. I was more determined to succeed in my attempt since I knew that others shared my convictions. The possibility of achieving financial independence was no longer just a faraway fantasy; it was materializing before my very eyes.

But I was fully aware of how brutal the business world could be. Challenges, setbacks, and unanticipated barriers lined the way to achievement. I understood that it was just the start of a journey that would be filled with both victories and sorrows, despite the fact that the support and excitement of investors were priceless.

The corporate environment may be harsh, always putting your flexibility and resilience to the test. It requires not just knowledge and enthusiasm but also the capacity to withstand hardship, come to difficult judgments, and change course when required. Armed with the awareness that achieving financial independence needed more than just having a fantastic concept, I was ready to take on these difficulties head-on. This required unflinching persistence and an unyielding conviction in the goal.

I brought the lessons I had learnt throughout my career with me as I delved further into the realm of business. The ability to forge connections, deliver value, and sell without selling were not only business-related talents; they served as my guiding principles in this new phase of my life. These ideas would form the basis for my quest toward financial security, together with the knowledge and assistance of investors.

The Highs and Lows of My Entrepreneurial Journey

My entrepreneurial path was an exhilarating rollercoaster of highs and lows, a frenzy of obstacles, excitement, and significant personal growth. I knew going into my journey for financial freedom that it wouldn't be an easy road.

The Highs

The moment my company idea began to take shape was one of the high points. A spark of inspiration was what started the fire inside of me.

I could see my business's potential, effect, and success in the long run. It was an exhilarating experience for me to see that idea come to life; it gave me motivation and drive.

Also, undoubtedly, gaining the support and capital of investors was a high point. It was confirmation that my idea had substance and that other people shared my enthusiasm for it. Their assistance gave us the tools we needed to make our goals come true. Undoubtedly, gaining the support and capital of investors was a high point. It was confirmation that my idea had substance and that other people shared my enthusiasm for it. Their assistance gave us the tools we needed to make our goals come true.

There were moments of early success when the company got off the ground that increased my confidence. Milestones that offered a sense of achievement included gratifying consumer feedback, rising revenue, and industry recognition.

The Lows

Early on, the financial burden of starting a business was very heavy. There were times when revenue fell short of projections and there was a lot of pressure to pay bills. It served as a sobering reminder that achieving financial independence remained a long way off. The dread of failure was a constant companion during the lows, there were sleepless hours spent worrying about the results of crucial decisions, and entrepreneurship is fundamentally unpredictable and risk is ever-present.

Personal sacrifices were necessary during the voyage, such as missing out on time with loved ones and delaying personal objectives. It was a constant struggle to strike a balance between the needs of the business and the desire for work-life harmony. It was unavoidable to have setbacks, which may range from a significant customer loss to unanticipated market adjustments. These lows put my fortitude to the test and made me adapt, sometimes in unexpected ways.

Chapter 6
I Was Ready to Do Whatever It Took

The way business was going wasn't as I had expected. Even though I was aware that the road to entrepreneurship wouldn't be easy, the reality was very different from my expectations. It seemed as though my years of marketing experience had failed me. But little did I realize that this trying time was only another season of learning, a furnace where tenacity and resolve would be formed.

As a business, we were in the red financially. Investors who had previously shown faith in our business were now dissatisfied and irate at the decline we were experiencing. The pressure of being in charge of the business weighed heavily on me. I was mentally exhausted from my constant hunt for the source of our issues. It was a challenging time that put my leadership and dedication to the absolute test.

My wife, Lucy, was my biggest source of hope and inspiration during this chaos. She never wavered in her support of me and gave me assurance when I needed it the most. During this turbulent time, leaving the office to see her was my daily solace and a reminder of what really important. Nevertheless, despite how consoling her presence was, I was aware that I had to do something to save our struggling company.

The shock of my life- The betrayal!

A shocking revelation, though, would make things much more difficult. My colleague Jimmy, whom I had thought to be a buddy, turned out to be a covert traitor. Jimmy has been working behind the scenes to undermine me since he quit his old job to work with me on this project. He was the root of the issues afflicting our business, launching an effort to undermine confidence in my leadership.

Jimmy had displayed an immense enthusiasm for the business, so his actions were especially puzzling. Because of his apparent commitment, I had even thought about giving him a directing position. It was upsetting to realize that someone

I had blindly trusted had turned against me, and it was clear from his actions that they were not in my best interests.

No matter what it took, I was going to change the story. The path ahead was difficult, but I stayed steadfast in my dedication to the company's success. I was prepared to go to any lengths to learn the full depth of Jimmy's treachery and resolve our financial problems.

The way forward

Our situation needed to be solved in many different ways. I started by conducting a detailed study of Jimmy's behavior to look for specific proof of his deception. Before taking any action against him, it was crucial to have unquestionable evidence.

I also concentrated on winning back the confidence of our investors. The basis of this work became open and honest communication. I met with them on a frequent basis, giving them honest updates on the situation, admitting our mistakes, and describing the actions we were doing to address the problems.

I also relied largely on my network of connections, which had served as a pillar of support throughout my career. I sought out mentors, colleagues in my field, and friends who might offer support and advice at this challenging period. Their knowledge and counsel were really helpful in resolving the problem.

The magnitude of Jimmy's betrayal became shockingly clear as we dug deeper into the inquiry. His actions had not only destroyed trust but also hurt our standing in the business. With the proof in hand, we took the appropriate legal steps to cut off contact with him and safeguard the business' interests.

It was difficult but not impossible to recover the company's finances and image. We started implementing cost-cutting strategies, improved our business processes, and redirected our marketing efforts. The investors, who had previously lost faith, started to restore it when they saw the practical measures, we were taking to right the ship.

Our effort and commitment eventually paid off. The business slowly but surely started to earn a profit. As we executed constructive adjustments and achieved excellent outcomes, our investors' faith was gradually reestablished.

Jimmy's actions effects on the organization's staff

Jimmy's betrayal had profound effects that went beyond our financial difficulties. His actions had a ripple effect across our company, harming the livelihoods and general wellbeing of our hardworking people.

Jimmy's deception caused the financial crisis to worsen, making it harder and harder to keep our current personnel. We were no longer able to keep a full crew due to the poor money earned during his term. It was a heartbreaking choice that I carried about on my shoulders.

Many of our employees had to confront the terrible reality of being let go. These were people who had put their faith in our company and devoted their time and skills to realizing our common goal. Knowing that their displacement was a result of our financial difficulties made it difficult to watch them depart.

In addition to those that were fired, several employees left of their own volition. They made the decision to go for more secure job elsewhere after sensing the burden of our financial difficulties. It was a loss for our team's cohesion and togetherness as much as for our skill.

I very clearly remember one of my mentors telling me that there would be times when I would feel lonely while working for financial freedom. This was one of those times, and it served as a sobering reminder of the loneliness that may come along with pursuing one's financial objectives.

The mood within the company has undergone a significant change. The lively and active workplace I had previously known was now characterized by empty desks and a palpable sense of uncertainty. Despite their resiliency, the surviving employees had to shoulder heavier workloads as they filled the voids left by their departing coworkers.

I felt a great feeling of duty and remorse as the gravity of this circumstance weighed heavily on me. I had failed to safeguard our staff members' livelihoods by giving a position of control to the incorrect individual. In terms of leadership and trust, it was a hard lesson.

My wife, Lucy, who continued to offer unwavering support, the mounting bills that reminded me of the necessity of finding a solution to our financial problems, and the unwavering vision I held for our business were the only sources of inspiration that remained constant amid the difficulties and the isolation that came with this season.

I couldn't even contemplate the idea that our business would fail. Our hopes for the business, its potential for growth, and the futures of the surviving employees all rested on its survival. I was resolved to do whatever it needed to get through these rough waters because I could not afford to fail.

My mental and emotional toughness had been put to the test throughout this difficult time, in addition to our financial fortitude. It was a humiliating event that emphasized the value of effective leadership, moral decision-making, and the requirement to safeguard the interests of individuals who relied on our organization.

A Risky Decision to Take

The grim reality of our business's dire financial situation was inescapable. The income had dwindled to a trickle, just enough to support the basic costs of the business. I had a sudden fall that gave me the impression that I was lost in the middle of a large, choppy ocean.

I had come to the point when I had tried every possible course. The several strategies and backup plan I had painstakingly created appeared to have fallen short in the face of our growing financial difficulties. It was a depressing situation, and the weight of the accountability I bore slammed in my chest.

We had investors' money involved in the company, which made the problem worse. These were people who had put their confidence and financial resources in our hands because they believed in the mission of our business. I could not stomach the idea of disappointing them, and I was determined to do all in my power to prevent it from happening.

Time was slipping through my fingers, and I knew I couldn't watch helplessly while our firm teetered on the verge of failure. It was a time when making a quick decision—some might even argue a hazardous one—was necessary.

I Gave My All

I didn't take the choice I made lightly. It was a calculated gamble that could either save our organization from certain disaster or drag it deeper into chaos. But I had no other alternative; I had to sacrifice everything I had in order to save the mission, the livelihoods of our employees, and the confidence of our investors.

I started by calling an urgent gathering of our investors. Transparency was crucial, and I had to express the seriousness of the problem while also outlining a clear course of action. The meeting was tense, and I felt the pressure of their expectations pressing in on me.

I described the stark truth of our financial difficulties, including the difficulties we had encountered and how they had affected how the business operated. It was challenging to have the talk, but it was crucial that our investors realized the seriousness of the issue.

Then, I offered a calculatedly hazardous proposal that involves using the company's remaining finances, including those of our investors, to make tactical investments with the potential to change the course of the situation. I was well aware of the risks involved because it was a high-stakes bet.

Our investors' reactions were conflicted. Some people were wary, rightly worried about the possibility of greater monetary loss. Others were cautiously hopeful and would support the strategy if it truly increased the likelihood of success.

We set out on a risky voyage with the support of a percentage of our investors. It entailed widening our product lineup, entering new markets, and making smart acquisitions. Success was far from assured, and the path ahead was paved with uncertainty.

It was not a hasty choice to take this risk. It was the result of thorough research, a deep conviction in the development potential, and a steadfast dedication to the mission of our business. I was willing to put everything on the line for this venture, giving it everything I had to make sure our company not only survived, but flourished.

Chapter 7

A Sigh of Relief

As I started a move that had the potential to completely transform our failing company, my heart was in my mouth. It was a risky choice, but it had the potential to change the course of events in our favor. Nothing less than entering the enormous and uncharted foreign market, which contained both promise and uncertainty, was decided upon.

I had little to no prior experience with commercial operations in the continent of Africa, which was the target for our international market. It was a risky decision that would put to the test both our adaptability and our fortitude in the face of the unknown. The stakes were quite high, and there was very little room for error.

We made the decision to send a small group of our employees to the African market to help us traverse this unfamiliar region. Their objective was quite clear: to carry out in-depth market research on the need for nutritional supplements for undernourished kids. This project wasn't only about growing our company; it also aimed to improve the lives of individuals who were less fortunate.

We wisely decided to hire licensed nutritionists specifically for this project since we were aware of the sensitive and complicated nature of the subject at hand. Understanding the special dietary requirements and difficulties experienced by malnourished children in the African environment would benefit greatly from their expertise.

We had a successful collaboration with these nutrition experts, one that was based on a common dedication to the purpose. Our team set out to do in-depth research under their direction, collecting information and market insights that would help us choose how to approach the African market.

We all sighed with relief when the reports from the field were finally received. The results were encouraging and showed that there was a real demand for the dietary supplement we wanted to offer. It provided the confirmation we were looking for, demonstrating that entering the

African market wasn't simply a hazardous bet but also a well-thought-out strategic decision.

We started working diligently for months to get ready for our entry into this new market. We were aware that the key to success would be careful preparation, paying close attention to detail, and having a thorough grasp of the cultural intricacies of the areas we would be working in.

From there, our recently recruited dietitians took over and started putting our plan into action. Collaboration efforts resulted in significant alliances with important players in the African nations we targeted. These alliances were crucial in easing our introduction into the market and ensuring that our dietary supplements got to people who needed them.

Our influence grew along with our market share in Africa. We developed become a key nutritional supplement provider, helping to address the crucial problem of childhood malnutrition. Our finances started to expand as a result of the measurable financial improvements, which was a welcome respite following the turbulent time we had just experienced.

Even though it was risky, the choice to enter the global market had paid dividends. It was a turning point in our quest for financial independence.

From Obscurity to Prosperity

Unexpectedly, a company endeavor we knew very little about at the beginning turned out to be our cash cow. Our path to financial freedom was significantly impacted by this unanticipated success story, which was fueled by a mix of imagination, ingenuity, and a never-ending eagerness to try new things.

It felt as though the floodgates of fortune had been unleashed as our company began to thrive. We had a sudden influx of money that changed our financial situation and gave us access to prospects we had only before dreamed of. Our investors, who had previously been skeptical and dissatisfied, were suddenly enthusiastic and upbeat about the course that our business was taking.

Our guiding ideals became ***innovation*** and ***creativity***. We were aware that *complacency* was the enemy of advancement in the dynamic world of business. We were adamant about staying in front of the curve, always looking for new methods to enhance our goods and services, and investigating cutting-edge approaches to satisfy the demands of our clients.

Our readiness to accept change and take reasonable chances was one of the distinguishing characteristics of our success. We were looking to grow and expand; we weren't satisfied with the way things were. This kind of thinking motivated us to investigate new markets, broaden our product line, and respond to changing trends.

As our company's success grew, we were given the chance to grow even more. We grabbed hold of it with both hands since it was a chance we had been looking forward to. The firm as well as our investors, who saw the possibility for even bigger returns, enthusiastically supported our growth efforts.

Finally, my life was moving in the direction I had long wanted it to. The desire of financial independence was now a concrete reality rather than an ideal. It was evidence of our determination, tenacity, and unwavering belief in our mission that had seen us through the most trying moments.

However, success has never been about money alone. I've always thought it's important to support struggling businesses and the community. It was time to put these ideals into practice with our newfound affluence. We were eager to improve mankind, not just via our goods and services but also through charitable endeavors.

Through collaborations that offered chances for development and sustainability, financial support, and mentorship programs, our dedication to helping struggling businesses took form. We were resolved to lend a helping hand to people traveling a similar path because we were aware of the difficulties encountered by entrepreneurs and had experienced our fair share of storms.

Also, we finally adopted the charitable attitude after realizing the significant positive influence it may have on the lives of the less fortunate. Whether it was assisting in disaster relief efforts, tackling healthcare inequities, or advancing issues important to our hearts, we developed projects to support them.

Beyond Broke

Conclusion

In our trip through the pages of "Beyond Broke: Empowering Your Finances in the Face of Bills," we looked at the transforming power of belief and the unyielding tenacity of the human spirit. We started our journey by accepting our financial situation and tackling the difficulties of having an empty wallet and mounting debt head-on. The core of empowerment rests in our ability to look beyond our constraints, even though the journey wasn't always simple and at times may have appeared impossible.

We stressed the critical part of mindset. It is the foundation upon which financial empowerment is based, not merely a trendy term. You are correct, whether you think you can or can't. Your ideas affect your reality, and this principle is especially true in the financial industry. We have experienced the incredible transition that takes place when we change our perspective from scarcity to plenty and from uncertainty to resolve as we have traveled this trip together.

As we come to an end on this empowering trip, keep in mind that financial empowerment is about ownership—ownership of your life, your decisions, and your destiny. The transformation from "broke" to "empowered" is a lifetime commitment to development, resiliency, and financial savvy rather than a destination.

Therefore, have faith in your ability to change the situation, control your financial future, and emerge not just stronger but also smarter. Although the road may be difficult, financial empowerment has immense benefits. Everything starts with one action, a mental shift, and the unyielding conviction that you can and will overcome financial difficulty. Your financial empowerment is in your hands, and the opportunities are endless. Take it with confidence as you continue your adventure.

*You too can become whatever
you picture in your mind.
I guarantee you!
Start Dreaming...*

www.ingramcontent.com/pod-product-compliance
Lightning Source LLC
Chambersburg PA
CBHW062250290526
45794CB00006B/2492